PROGENY

When You Grow Up You Can be Anything That You Want To Be

artwork by: Ronald Carter

RONALD CARTER

To order additional copies of this book, contact:
Xlibris
844-714-8691
www.Xlibris.com
Orders@Xlibris.com

ISBN: Softcover   978-1-6698-5871-3
        EBook   978-1-6698-5870-6

Print information available on the last page

Rev. date: 12/06/2022

Foreword

I enjoy existing and participating in the world of the arts, history, and the literary domain. It allows me the chance of self-expression while experiencing the world from multiple perspectives and meeting many intriguing and interesting personalities. I was always pushed to achieve goals in life that were reasonably attainable. I was shown that through hard work and much effort, I could become anything that I wanted to be. I have had my setbacks, but that is okay. With those setbacks, I regrouped and kept it moving forward, perhaps with some regrets. I was able to pick myself up and dust myself off, keeping a positive mind and accomplishing my goals while bringing some of my dreams to fruition. That is what this book is about—inspiration and bringing dreams to life.

Because of the experiences of African Americans in America, many of our black children have dreams that are broken, destroyed, and stepped on by the evilness of others. This book will show them that their dreams are real and can come true. Young African American children can succeed by becoming anything that they want to be, from bricklayer to president of the United States. With dedicated work and study, when they grow up, they can become anything that they want to be, and you can take that to the bank.

This book is dedicated to my children, Gunya, Sunya, George, Torey, Crystal, and Gaynelle; grandchildren, Christopher, Tiara, Destiny, Taquane, Damon, Bahira, Sean, Kaijin, Kya, Khyrel, Lanae, Hassani, Dana, Jakwon, Aubrey, Jet, and Chyanne; and my great-grandchildren, Laurece, Isaam, Amori, Jordyn, Jayce, Taquane Jr., Jayden, Lauren, Raylan, and Emani,

My children, grandchildren, and great-grandchildren, including the art group Progeny's Legacy Jamaa, depicting two storytellers telling stories to a family of children and parents, are part of the inspiration for this book. Enjoy!

Yes! My children, you are the progeny, the future of our generations to come. You are the recipients of the stories told by the village griots. Stories from these storytellers are the histories going back generations upon generations into the past, celebrating your ancestors. You possess the knowledge and intelligence of the universe. You are the children who will grow up to become anything you wish to be. From bricklayers to scientists and beyond, you can become anything you want to be. "You are the progeny's legacy jamaa!"

Hi! My name is North Philly. Like me, when you grow up, you can become anything you want to be.

Yes! When you grow up, you can become a
doctor or a nurse, even a medical technician.

Hey! Hey! My name is Groove, and like me, if you go to school and graduate, when you grow up, you can become anything that you want to be.

Oh my! When you grow up, you can become
a lawyer or a judge, even a paralegal.

Hello there! My name is Bolo, and like me, if you study hard and do your homework, when you grow up, you can become anything that you want to be.

Oh yeah! You can grow up to become the president or vice president of the United States. You can become a congressman, or even a senator. Just think! You can even become a city council person, mayor, or even a governor.

Hello, my friends! My name is Yo, and like me and my brothers North Philly, Groove, and Bolo, when you grow up, you can become anything that you want to be.

You can grow up to become a professional tennis player, a professional football player, or even a professional baseball player, and yes, a professional soccer player too.

Hi there! If you work hard and get good grades in school, you can become anything that you want to be.

And when you grow up, you can also have a family
with a warm, loving home full of love and fun.

Never forget that you can become
anything that you want to be.

You can grow up to become a professional
basketball player, earning the respect of others.

When you grow up, you can become
anything that you want to be.

You can become a musician, an artist, or a writer of short stories and poetry. While you are young, you can learn to sing, play the trumpet, play the guitar, or learn to play other musical instruments.

It is fun to have a good laugh now and then. Laughter is good for you and others. Laughter makes everyone happy.

When you are happy, you can go to school, feeling good about yourself. You can study and do classroom assignments and homework. These are some of the things that help you to become anything that you want to be when you grow up.

Remember that when you grow up, you can
become anything that you want to be.

You can become a schoolteacher or a college professor when you grow up. Believe me. This is true.

Believe in yourself and become anything
that you want to become in your life.

You can become an astronaut, traveling through space and time, visiting the stars, and exploring the unknown.

When you grow up, you can become
anything that you want to be.

You can become a dancer, conga and djembe player, or even a trap drum musician. In the world of rhythms, it is always possible.

Run, laugh, and play, as children always do.
One day, you may become what you want to
be with fun, happiness, and laughter.

Never let anyone tell you what you cannot be, crushing your dreams. Fight from within yourself to become what you want to be when you grow up. Follow your dreams that they may come true.

Say no to drugs, guns, and violence!

You can become anything that you
want to be when you grow up.

You can become a police officer, firefighter, or military soldier when you grow up. These are the choices that you may make for yourself.

Remember that you can become anything, or whatever you want to be, when you grow up.

Please understand that you are a unique person. No one can decide for you what you want to be when you grow up. That is a personal choice for you and you alone. Follow your heart, follow your skills, and follow your dreams. Believe in yourself and be proud. When you grow up, you can be anything that you want to be.

Peace, love, blessings, and prosperity.

Printed in the United States
by Baker & Taylor Publisher Services